Magical Milk

Written by **Nasheeda Pollard**
Illustrated by **Katura Gaines**

Dedicated to you unapologetically defining your journey,
no matter what that may look like.

Visit lactationgoddess.com to learn more about our products and services.
Instagram @lactationgoddess

Meet my new **baby sister!**

Mom feeds her **breast milk**
for breakfast, lunch, and dinner.

My sister can't talk yet so she gives us **clues**.

She'll turn her head or lick her lips when she wants **magical milk food**.

A very special recipe made just for her tiny tummy.

Yellow and **white** to name a few.

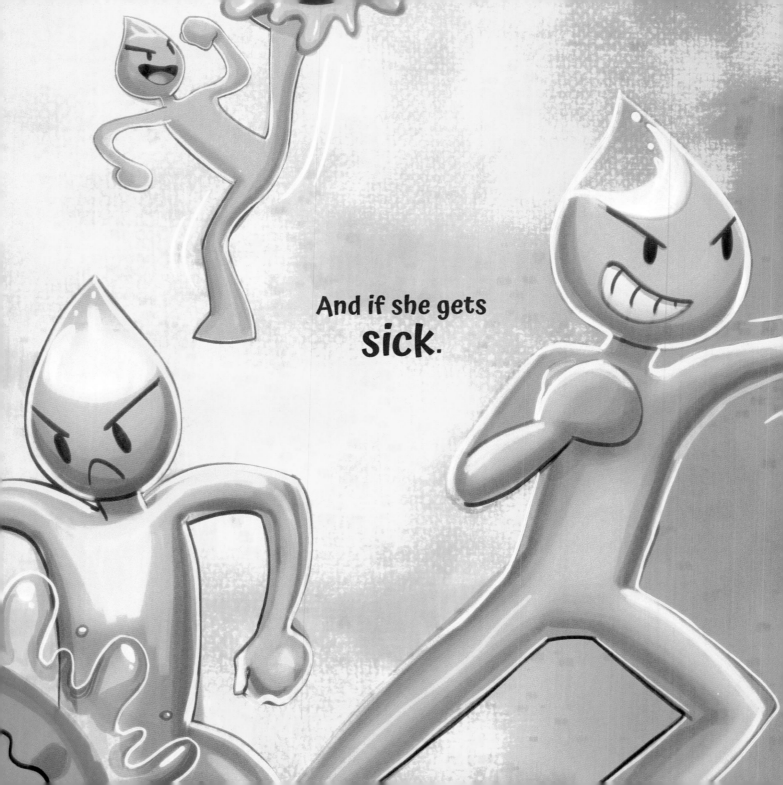

And if she gets **sick**.

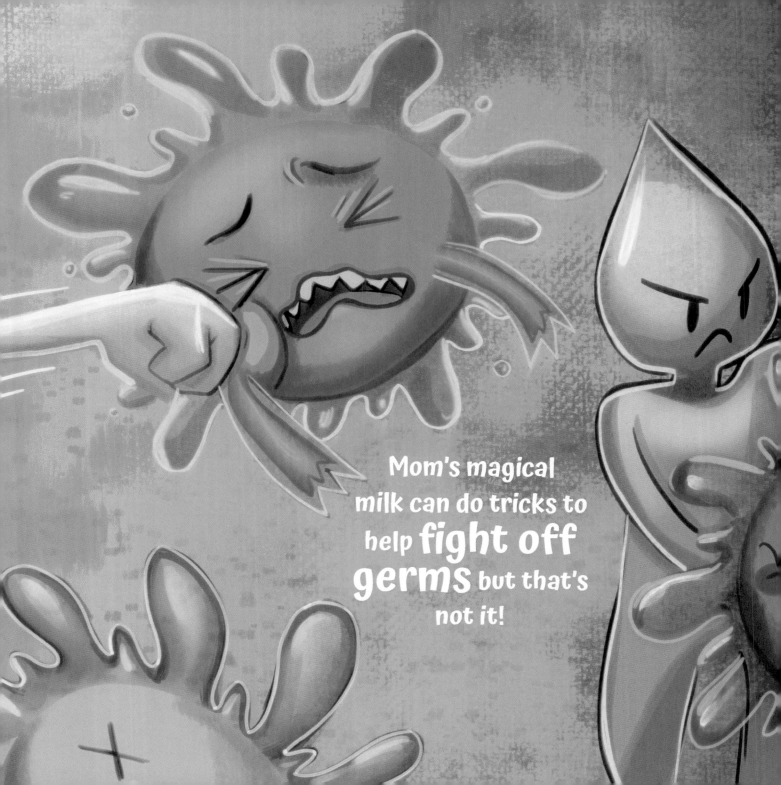

Hey, did you know magical milk
helps babies grow?

Healthy and strong from head to toe!

Some **vitamins** here and **minerals** there. Good stuff sprinkled everywhere!

Dad thinks magical milk is cool too because of the things it **can do**.

You can use it in a bath or in my baby sister's hair...

this milk is so good.

It can be used almost anywhere!

Milk in bottles, milk in breasts,
milk in funny shaped necklaces.
Milk for one or for two.
Magical milk for toddlers too!

You can make milk **popsicles** or *ice cream*. Magical milk can be used for many things!

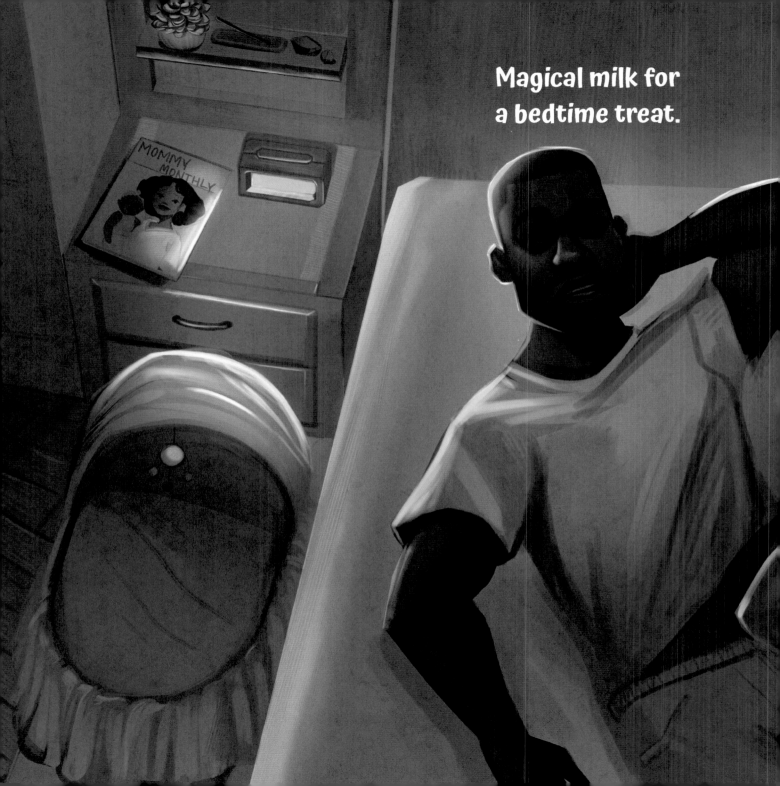

Magical milk for
a bedtime treat.

Warm and **sweet.**
It helps her sleep.

For days, weeks, or months. This milk is **golden**!

No matter where we are,
in a store or in a car.

Magical milk is there waiting. It's never too far.

This milk is magical.
Yes, indeed!

Copyright © 2022 by Nasheeda Pollard.

To request permissions, contact us at info@lactationgoddess.com

ISBN: 978-1-7376890-0-3 (paperback)
ISBN: 978-1-7376890-1-0 (hardcover)

Library of Congress Control Number: 2022908860

Illustrator Katura Gaines
Layout by Sara Paz
First printed June 2022